Let's Remember Your Baptism

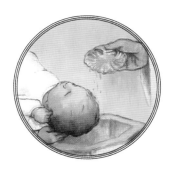

Let's Remember Your Baptism

Readings, Memories, and Records of a Special Day

Paraclete Press
Brewster, Massachusetts

2021 First Printing

Let's Remember Your Baptism: Readings, Memories, and Records of a Special Day
by Paraclete Press

Copyright © 2021 by Paraclete Press

ISBN 978-1-64060-590-9

The Paraclete Press name and logo (dove on cross) are trademarks of
Paraclete Press, Inc.

Library of Congress Cataloging-in-Publication Data

Title: Let's remember your baptism : readings, memories, and records of a
special day.
Description: Brewster, Massachusetts : Paraclete Press, 2020. | Summary: "A
beautifully illustrated book with pages to record memories of this
  special day"– Provided by publisher.
Identifiers: LCCN 2020017928 | ISBN 9781640605909 (hardcover)
Subjects: LCSH: Infant baptism–Juvenile literature.
Classification: LCC BV813.3 .L48 2020 | DDC 265/.12–dc23
LC record available at https://lccn.loc.gov/2020017928

10 9 8 7 6 5 4 3 2 1

Published by Paraclete Press
Brewster, Massachusetts
www.paracletepress.com

Manufactured By Regent Publishing Services Limited, Hong Kong.
Printed September, 2020, in ShenZhen, Guangdong, China.

This child has been reborn in Baptism.

This is now a child of God.

Presentation Page

This book is for _____.
(full Christian/baptismal name here)

This is the gift of _____.

You were baptized on this day: _____.

In this church: _____.

Contents

The Calling of the Baptized

I therefore . . . beg you to lead a life worthy of the calling to which you have been called, with all humility and gentleness, with patience, bearing with one another in love, making every effort to maintain the unity of the Spirit in the bond of peace.

There is one body and one Spirit, just as you were called to the one hope of your calling, one Lord, one faith, one baptism, one God and Father of all, who is above all and through all and in all.

—St. Paul the Apostle
Ephesians 4:1–6

Family members and friends who were present at your Baptism

(Allow people to print and sign their names here,
followed by a short message.)

_____

_____

_____

_____

_____

A Prayer

Dear God,
You have called each of us to know and love you,
to live our lives in your service.
Surround this child today and always with your
everlasting and abiding love.
Protect this child from evil, and fill him/her with
your Holy Spirit, as he/she is received into
your holy Church.
Together, by your grace, we will walk in love together,
and continue to grow in your love.
Amen.

The Responsibilities of Family and Friends

(Read this aloud, if possible, when everyone is together.)

WE ARE TO DO THESE THINGS

"Train children in the right way,
and when old, they will not stray."
—*Proverbs 22:6*

Be thoughtfully involved in their lives—even if from afar.

Be physically present, whenever possible,
at other important moments.

Pray. Pray.

A Psalm of David

The LORD is my light and my salvation;
   whom shall I fear?
The LORD is the stronghold of my life;
   of whom shall I be afraid?

One thing I asked of the LORD,
   that will I seek after:
to live in the house of the LORD
   all the days of my life,
to behold the beauty of the LORD,
   and to inquire in his temple.

For he will hide me in his shelter
　　in the day of trouble;
he will conceal me under the cover of his tent;
　　he will set me high on a rock.

I believe that I shall see the goodness of the LORD
　　in the land of the living.
Wait for the LORD;
　　be strong, and let your heart take courage;
　　wait for the LORD!

—Psalm 27:1, 4, 5, 13–14

The Baptism of Our Lord

I n those days Jesus came from Nazareth of Galilee and was baptized by John in the Jordan. And just as he was coming up out of the water, he saw the heavens torn apart and the Spirit descending like a dove on him. And a voice came from heaven, "You are my Son, the Beloved; with you I am well pleased."

—*Mark 1:9–11*

Jesus Blesses Little Children

People were bringing little children to him in order that he might touch them; and the disciples spoke sternly to them. But when Jesus saw this, he was indignant and said to them, "Let the little children come to me; do not stop them; for it is to such as these that the kingdom of God belongs. Truly I tell you, whoever does not receive the kingdom of God as a little child will never enter it." And he took them up in his arms, laid his hands on them, and blessed them.

—Mark 10:13–16

A Message from Your Parents on This Day

A Parents' Prayer

Dear God, we thank and praise you this day.

Thank you for our child.

Thank you for your Church.

Thank you for our family.

Thank you for our friends.

Thank you for this gift of Holy Baptism.

Show us, Lord, each day, how best to guide our child.
Give us the grace to teach our child your ways.
Make clear to us the path we all should follow.
We want our family to walk in holiness.
May we be worthy of our calling as your children—
As children of God.
Amen.

"Every baptized person should consider that it is in the womb of the Church where he is transformed from a child of Adam to a child of God."

—St. Vincent Ferrer

Our Wish for You...

SEEK GOD'S WILL
"Jesus, help me to simplify my life
by learning what you want me to be—
and becoming that person."

—ST. THÉRÈSE OF LISIEUX

FIND YOUR HAPPINESS

"You will never be happy if your happiness depends on getting solely what you want. Change the focus. Get a new center. Will what God wills, and your joy no man shall take from you."

—VENERABLE FULTON J. SHEEN

BE COURAGEOUS

"The ultimate measure of a man is not where he stands in moments of comfort and convenience, but where he stands at times of challenge and controversy."

—DR. MARTIN LUTHER KING, JR.

BE WISE AND SMART

"Never mistake knowledge for wisdom. One helps you make a living. The other helps you make a life."

—ELEANOR ROOSEVELT

Just as a person can't live in the flesh unless he is born in the flesh, so one cannot have the spiritual life of grace unless he or she is born again spiritually. This regeneration is effected by Baptism: 'No one can enter the kingdom of God without being born of water and Spirit.'" (*John 3:5*)

—ST. THOMAS AQUINAS

Symbols of Baptism

THE CROSS

Making the sign of the cross over the baby during Baptism is a sign of God's protection, and an expression of faith and desire to be a part of the People of God.

WATER

A symbol of purity and cleansing, water is an ancient element of God's Creation. And with water, Jesus was baptized by John the Baptist in the Jordan River. *(See Matthew, chapter 3)*

OIL

This is a symbol of the Holy Spirit in many sacraments and ritual settings. To anoint the child with oil is to unite the child and God.

We Will Remember This Day

(Parents, write your thoughts here. Then review these pages later
with your child when he or she begins to read.)

1. Who was present at your Baptism, and will remain a
   central part of your life?

   _____

   _____

   _____

2. What will you remember most about that special day?

   _____

   _____

   _____

❀ 27 ❀

3. Was there a prayer, a Scripture verse, or a sentence from the Baptism ritual that stuck with you? Why?

_____

_____

_____

4. Did this Baptism cause you to think differently about, or plan anew for, your family?

_____

_____

_____

_____

Baptism Blessings

The LORD bless you and keep you.
The LORD make his face to shine upon you,
and be gracious to you.
The LORD lift up his countenance upon you,
and give you peace.

Numbers 6:24–26

Heavenly Father,
thank you for the precious gift of Baptism.
Thank you that we may publicly declare our love
and passion for you in this way.
Father, we ask that your grace and blessings
will be poured out on this faithful servant of yours.
Christ, we pray that you will work deeply
within his/her heart and soul,
conforming it to your own.
And Holy Spirit, we pray that you will come now
and guide his/her footsteps,
each and every day.

Come to us, Lord, Father of all.
Come to us by means of this holy water,
which you have created,
so that all who are baptized in it
may be washed clean of sin.
Come to us, we ask you, Lord,
that we may all be born again to live
as your children.

Father, through these waters of Baptism
you have filled us with new life
as your very own children.
Thank you.

From all who are baptized in water
and the Holy Spirit,
you have formed one people,
united in your Son, Jesus Christ.
Thank you.

You have set us all free
and filled our hearts with your love,
so that we may live in your peace.
Thank you.

You have called us to announce the Good News
of Jesus Christ to people everywhere,
by word and deed.
Thank you.

May the road rise up to meet you.
May the wind be always at your back.
May the sun shine warm upon your face,
the rains fall soft upon your fields,
and until we meet again,
may God hold you in the palm of his hand.

Traditional Irish Blessing

I lift up my eyes to the hills—
from where will my help come?
My help comes from the LORD,
who made heaven and earth.
He will not let your foot be moved;
he who keeps you will not slumber.
The LORD will keep
your going out and your coming in
from this time on and forevermore.

Psalm 121:1–3, 8

The Reason for Baptism

What then are we to say? Should we continue in sin in order that grace may abound? By no means! How can we who died to sin go on living in it? Do you know that all of us who have been baptized into Christ Jesus were baptized in his death?

Therefore we have been buried with him by baptism into death, so that, just as Christ was raised from the dead by the glory of the Father, so we too might walk in newness of life.

PAUL

Romans 6:1–4

About the Illustrator

Rebecca Lussier has enjoyed the creative energy and camaraderie shared among the artists at the Community of Jesus on Cape Cod for more than thirty years. Accomplished in a variety of media, she finds oil painting her latest joy. When not at her easel, she is most often found with her husband, Brad, enjoying yet another walk with their Brittany, Rustle.

Sources

About Paraclete Press

WHO WE ARE

As the publishing arm of the Community of Jesus, Paraclete Press presents a full expression of Christian belief and practice—from Catholic to Evangelical, from Protestant to Orthodox, reflecting the ecumenical charism of the Community and its dedication to sacred music, the fine arts, and the written word. We publish books, recordings, sheet music, and video/DVDs that nourish the vibrant life of the church and its people.

WHAT WE ARE DOING

Books | PARACLETE PRESS BOOKS show the richness and depth of what it means to be Christian. While Benedictine spirituality is at the heart of who we are and all that we do, our books reflect the Christian experience across many cultures, time periods, and houses of worship.

We have many series, including *Paraclete Essentials*; *Paraclete Fiction*; *Paraclete Poetry*; *Paraclete Giants*; and for children and adults, *All God's Creatures*, books about animals and faith; and *San Damiano Books*, focusing on Franciscan spirituality. Others include *Voices from the Monastery* (men and women monastics writing about living a spiritual life today), *Active Prayer*, and new for young readers: *The Pope's Cat*. We also specialize in gift books for children on the occasions of Baptism and First Communion, as well as other important times in a child's life, and books that bring creativity and liveliness to any adult spiritual life.

The MOUNT TABOR BOOKS series focuses on the arts and literature as well as liturgical worship and spirituality; it was created in conjunction with the Mount Tabor Ecumenical Centre for Art and Spirituality in Barga, Italy.

Music | PARACLETE PRESS DISTRIBUTES RECORDINGS of the internationally acclaimed choir *Gloriæ Dei Cantores*, the *Gloriæ Dei Cantores Schola*, and the other instrumental artists of the *Arts Empowering Life Foundation*.

PARACLETE PRESS IS THE EXCLUSIVE NORTH AMERICAN DISTRIBUTOR for the Gregorian chant recordings from St. Peter's Abbey in Solesmes, France. Paraclete also carries all of the Solesmes chant publications for Mass and the Divine Office, as well as their academic research publications.

In addition, PARACLETE PRESS SHEET MUSIC publishes the work of today's finest composers of sacred choral music, annually reviewing over 1,000 works and releasing between 40 and 60 works for both choir and organ.

Video | Our video/DVDs offer spiritual help, healing, and biblical guidance for a broad range of life issues including grief and loss, marriage, forgiveness, facing death, understanding suicide, bullying, addictions, Alzheimer's, and Christian formation.

Learn more about us at our website:
www.paracletepress.com
or phone us toll-free at 1.800.451.5006

SCAN
TO
READ

You may also be interested in these...

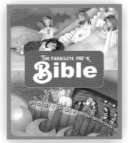

The Paraclete Pre-K Bible

ISBN 978-1-64060-619-7
Board book | $16.99

The Little Angels Book of Prayers

ISBN 978-1-61261-853-1
Hardcover | $9.99

My First Holy Communion

ISBN 978-1-55725-696-6
Hardcover | $14.99

Available at bookstores
Paraclete Press | 1-800-451-5006
www.paracletepress.com